COMMUNICATING WITH **CONFIDENCE**™

LISTEN UP

KNOWING WHEN AND WHEN NOT TO SPEAK

GREG ROZA

ROSEN
PUBLISHING®

New York

Published in 2012 by The Rosen Publishing Group, Inc.
29 East 21st Street, New York, NY 10010

First Edition

Library of Congress Cataloging-in-Publication Data

Roza, Greg.
Listen up : knowing when and when not to speak / Greg Roza. — 1st ed.
    p. cm. — (Communicating with confidence)
Includes bibliographical references and index.
ISBN 978-1-4488-5515-5 (library binding) — ISBN 978-1-4488-5516-2 (pbk.) —
ISBN 978-1-4488-5517-9 (6-pack)
1. Listening — Juvenile literature. I. Title.
BF323.L5R69 2011
153.6'8 — dc22
                                                    2011012008

Manufactured in the United States of America

CPSIA Compliance Information: Batch #W12YA: For further information, contact Rosen Publishing, New York, New York, at 1-800-237-9932.

CONTENTS

INTRODUCTION

Most people like to think they're good listeners. The people close to them, however, might think otherwise. Listening isn't always as simple as it sounds. Some people are surprised to hear that it's not simply remaining silent while another person is speaking. Listening is an interactive process involving both speaker and listener.

It can be difficult to listen to others when our own thoughts and impulses get in the way. Everyone has something they want to say, yet this can obstruct our ability to listen when others are speaking. Whether we realize it or not, many of us are planning what we want to say next instead of listening to the other person. This is one of the most common roadblocks to effective listening.

Other times the topic a speaker is telling us about reminds us of our own experiences. We quickly respond with our own stories. We usually mean well, hoping to empathize with the other person. Regardless of our intentions, however, once we start speaking, we're no longer listening. This can have the effect of pushing others away. They many stop sharing their thoughts with us if they think we're just going to start talking about ourselves.

Everyone needs someone to talk to from time to time. However, it's listening that makes relationships stronger.

Here's an example: One day after school, Marcus tells his dad, James, that he's having trouble with his math teacher. He's trying hard to keep up with the rest of the class, but he's falling behind. Furthermore, his teacher is getting annoyed with Marcus, which is making it harder for him to catch up. Before Marcus can finish, James tells his son that when he was in school, he hated English. But he stuck with it, worked as hard as he could, and ended up with a passing grade. "Stick with it," he tells his son, "you'll do fine."

While James might have the best intentions in telling Marcus a similar story from his past, he fails to truly listen to his son and hear his problem. Maybe math isn't Marcus's problem; perhaps he's not getting along with his math teacher. Or, maybe Marcus just needs someone to listen to him so that he can figure out what he needs to do on his own. By not listening—truly listening—James may have made Marcus's problem worse, despite his good intentions. Marcus may not come to his dad the next time he needs to talk.

Whether it's telling a parent about a good grade on a test, getting advice from a coworker about your job, or revealing a nagging fear to a good friend, everyone needs someone to talk to from time to time. Being a good listener helps build solid, meaningful relationships with people. Listening shows others that they matter to us. In the end, this pays off for both speaker and listener. The more time we spend truly listening to others, the more people there will be to listen to us when we need someone to talk to.

WHY IS LISTENING IMPORTANT?

Our listening skills affect many areas of our lives—from home, to school, to work. In short, there's always someone to listen to. Everybody needs to be heard. Think about how frustrating it can be when you have something important to say, but there's no one to listen to you. This can make us feel unappreciated, annoyed, depressed, and sometimes just plain lonely. When we have someone to talk to, we feel content, respected, and important. We also know that we have a true confidant.

It takes two people to have a conversation, and others need to be heard just as badly as we do. It can be hard to stop talking

Friends have the potential to be some of our best listeners. Show your friends you care by listening to them, and they're bound to become your true confidant.

and listen, but it's usually harder to turn off the sound of our own voice inside our head. The number one skill poor listeners need to learn is to stop thinking about themselves (and what they're going to say next), and instead pay attention to the person to whom they're listening. Being a good listener is kind to others, but it's also rewarding to ourselves. When you make the effort to listen to other people, other people will make the effort to listen to you.

Getting the Point

At its most basic level, listening allows us to understand the ideas and emotions others are trying to convey. When we don't listen, we miss important information. This can have a negative impact on many areas of our lives. A daughter who doesn't hear her mother tell her what time to be home after a movie may end up getting grounded. A father who doesn't hear his son say what time he needs to be picked up after the soccer game might find an angry kid when he finally does get there. Students surely won't pass a test if they fail to listen to the teacher during class. Football players who don't listen to the coach during practice probably won't get a lot of playing time during a game.

Listening skills are crucial for success when planning a career or when starting a new job. An employee who doesn't listen to the boss may not receive the raise or promotion he or she was hoping for. Worse yet, the employee may lose the job altogether. Employees who listen carefully understand assignments and the results expected of them. Effective on-the-job listening

Listening in the workplace shows respect for the boss, but it also helps you gather the information necessary to do the best job you can.

helps build positive relationships that benefit coworkers, managers, clients, and customers. It also allows workers to solve problems and create a productive working environment.

Good listeners "get it." They work to understand what others are saying. Furthermore, they use that knowledge to build positive relationships and achieve success in all areas of life. When it comes to communication skills, listening well is as essential as speaking and writing well.

Showing Respect

Has anyone ever dismissively said "Yeah, yeah" to you when you were trying to say something? How did it make you feel? Being interrupted or having our words dismissed can be maddening. On the other hand, patiently listening to another person is perceived as a sign of respect, which helps build lasting relationships. When people know you respect them, they will respect you back. They'll also be more likely to listen to you in your time of need.

In the business world, respect is key to getting ahead. An employer who doesn't respect you isn't likely to promote you. Likewise, coworkers who don't respect you are likely to mistrust you. Learning to listen to coworkers and bosses is the best way to earn their respect.

Listening also shows your fondness for the people closest to you. Personal relationships are based on mutual feelings of trust, respect, and compassion. It's impossible to build close personal relationships based on these concepts without actually listening to people.

Listening conveys our emotions and admiration for others, whether it's the love we feel for friends and family or the respect we have for our colleagues, bosses, and teachers. Sometimes we don't have to tell people we care for them, as long as we listen with a concerned ear. The people who talk to us need to be confident that they won't be judged, ignored, blamed, interrupted, or advised. Gaining respect and affection by being a good listener is an important part of forming a bond of trust between two individuals. And trust is an essential component of any relationship, whether it's personal or professional.

Listening to Problems

It can be troubling when we're worried about something and have no one to talk to. Keeping feelings such as sadness, remorse, loss, and guilt bottled up inside makes us feel worse. When we decide to open up to a friend, we usually feel much better just having shared our problem with him or her.

Some people feel compelled to say comforting words to a friend who comes to them with a problem. But this isn't always what the friend is looking for, and comforting words often sound hollow and cliché. Consider the following example. Jason notices that his friend Aaron seems depressed. Being a concerned friend, Jason asks him what's wrong. However, Jason isn't truly listening to Aaron.

Jason: What's wrong? You seem upset.

Aaron: My dog Cosmo is sick. My dad said he may not make it through the week. I can't imagine what I'll do without him. He's always been there for me.

Jason: Everything will be all right, you'll see. Don't be so sad. Let's go to the mall to take your mind off of it.

Jason thinks that by taking Aaron's mind off of his problem, he can cheer him up. But he doesn't do what a good friend needs to do in a situation like this—listen. Jason failed to recognize Aaron's need to confide in someone. Instead of listening, Jason cut Aaron off and changed the subject, leaving Aaron feeling sad and discontented. It's therapeutic to open up and talk about our feelings. But if there's no one to listen to us, we can end up feeling worse. By saying something like, "Don't worry, it'll get better," the speaker may feel the listener is brushing him or her off and avoiding listening to the problem.

As a good listener, it isn't always necessary to give advice to friends in need. They might not be looking for that. They might simply need for you to hear their problem. Simply listening to a friend in need allows him or her to find comfort from problems. A trusted friend needs to know that he or she won't be judged, blamed, interrupted, or advised. And when someone really is a good listener, the person's friends will be more likely to ask for advice in their time of need.

Sharing Good News

Just as people need to talk about their negative feelings and problems, we get a boost when we share our positive feelings. Whether someone is talking about a good grade, landing a dream job, or getting a part in the school play, it's healthy to talk about our accomplishments. Good listeners hear the speaker's joy without interrupting or relating it to their own experiences.

Sarah comes home from school with some news she's very proud of: she was selected to be a photographer for the school yearbook. She runs in to tell her mother—a professional photographer—the great news. If Sarah's mother was a bad listener, the conversation might go like this:

> **Sarah:** I can't believe it! They chose me to take photographs for the yearbook!

> **Mom:** Wow, that's great! I remember when I was in school, I took photos for the yearbook and the school newspaper. Keep trying and I bet you could get on the newspaper, too.

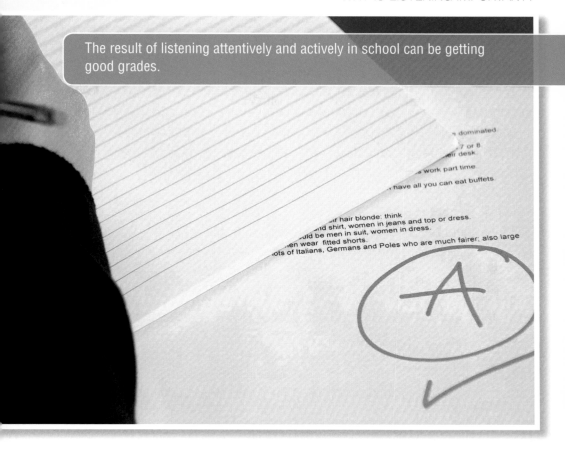

The result of listening attentively and actively in school can be getting good grades.

Sarah's mom is probably just trying to be supportive while encouraging her daughter to be the best photographer she can be. However, she seems to have missed the point. Sarah was not looking for advice on how to be a better photographer. Nor did she want her mom to compare their experiences. Rather, she was hoping to share some good news with someone she's close to. Sarah might decide not to share her accomplishments with her mom if she continues to be a bad listener. Sometimes all we need to hear is "Great job!" to know someone is proud of us.

Are You a Good Listener?

We'd all like to think we're good listeners, but how do we really know if we are? We can only become good at listening through practice. The skills in this book are intended to help readers do just that.

Part of being a good listener is being able to identify both good and bad habits.

Bad Habits	Good Habits
glancing frequently at your watch	maintaining eye contact with the speaker
yawning	nodding and smiling
interrupting to ask questions	waiting for the speaker to pause to ask questions
playing with your jewelry, glasses, or cell phone	sitting or standing still
judging speakers before they have a chance to speak	allowing a speaker to finish talking before judging his or her words
failing to verify the meaning behind a speaker's words	repeating what the speaker says in new words to verify the meaning

Yawning while listening is a bad habit because it implies that you're bored or you don't care. If you can't avoid yawning, apologize to the speaker and encourage him or her to continue.

What Do You Really Mean?

In their book, *Are You Really Listening? Keys to Successful Communication*, Paul J. Donoghue and Mary E. Siegel say, "When someone listens to us, we are given the opportunity to hear ourselves." What they mean is that when we speak to a good listener, it allows us to hear our thoughts spoken out loud. This gives us a chance to evaluate our thoughts and clarify what we believe. Sometimes all a speaker is looking for is a chance to vocalize his or her thoughts and come to a better understanding about how he or she feels. Some people refer to this as being a "sounding board" for someone else.

Even those people who have many listeners, such as public speakers and radio hosts, need to listen to their audience to communicate effectively.

There are good things to be said about offering friends advice or telling them a personal story to help show your understanding of what they're saying. However, good listeners need to remember that a speaker isn't necessarily looking for those things. Advice and personal stories can have a negative effect on someone simply trying to use a friend as a sounding board. Switching the conversation to our own thoughts and feelings can also make the speaker feel cut off, underappreciated, and misunderstood. The speaker may become confused about what he or she really feels.

As good listeners, we need to put ourselves into the mind of the speaker, get behind her words, and allow the person to express herself before offering advice. The speaker may eventually ask for your opinion, but in the end, she might be able to figure out how she feels simply by getting it off her chest.

Life Listening

Listening is important for many reasons. Perhaps it can best be summed up by saying that listening builds strong, long-lasting relationships. At home, listening helps us grow closer to those we love. Listening allows us to excel at school. It also helps us to do well at work. In this book, you'll learn the essential listening skills needed to get closer to those around you and be successful in all you do.

CHAPTER 2

THE OBSTACLES TO GOOD LISTENING

There's a lot for us to listen to every day: the alarm clock, cereal being poured into a bowl, the school bus's brakes squealing as it stops in front of a house.

But just because we hear something, does it mean that we're truly listening? A common trap for bad listeners is not actually using their brains to process the words they're hearing. Most people will admit that there are times when they missed what a person was saying, even though they were both participating in the same conversation. This happens more often for bad listeners.

Sometimes it can be difficult not to daydream at school. Good listeners find ways to stay focused and ready to learn.

What could stop someone from truly hearing what another person is saying? The reasons we don't hear people can be hard to recognize at first. Once we understand the various obstacles to effective listening, we can apply them to our own experiences. This allows us to identify our listening weaknesses, improve our communication skills, and forge lasting relationships.

Oftentimes you'll hear parents complaining that their kids don't listen. Kids often complain that their parents don't listen. However, both sides need to practice good listening skills to solve family disputes.

Lack of Focus

Have you ever been in a class during a lecture and realized that you had been daydreaming instead of taking notes? Has a friend ever said, "So what do you think?" only to realize you had been thinking about something other than his words? It happens to everyone. No matter how hard we want to listen, our minds drift. This lack of focus is one of the most common forms of bad listening.

Losing focus can result in a bad grade at school, a disappointed parent at home, or an angry boss at work. As good listeners, we need to train ourselves to pay attention when others are talking.

You Talk Too Much

Chances are if you're talking, you're not hearing what others are saying. Even when our mouths are closed, however, our voices continue to talk inside our heads. It's inevitable. We're so used to listening to our own thoughts that they sometimes influence the way we interpret the words of others. Even as someone else starts talking, our opinions are shaping what we think about what he or she is saying.

In his book *The 7 Habits of Highly Effective People*, Stephen R. Covey writes, "Most people do not listen with the intent to understand; they listen with the intent to reply." Many people are guilty of planning what they'll say when the speaker has finished talking,

In addition to writing books, Dr. Stephen R. Covey also gives lectures and workshops to teach people how to be successful in life.

instead of listening closely. We often begin talking the instant the other person pauses. It's natural to want to contribute to the conversation, but when we plan out what we want to say next, we aren't focusing on the speaker. If there's something you feel you really need to say, try jotting it down and bring it up later when the speaker has finished.

Being Defensive

Bad listeners sometimes believe they're being criticized or attacked, whether they really are or not. Instead of carefully

Being defensive and refusing to listen to others is a sure way to damage valuable friendships.

listening for the speaker's real meaning, they hear accusations and then go on the defensive. This type of response could be the result of insecurity or an irrational effort to protect themselves from an attack. The listener may respond by attacking back or by trying to make the speaker feel guilty for criticizing him or her.

Defensiveness can cause problems in our personal and professional lives. For example, during a meeting at work, Jake's boss, Sam, gives him some suggestions for increasing his sales and earning more money. Sam thinks Jake is a promising salesman and wants to give him some advice to help him improve. However, Jake feels like Sam is criticizing his work. Jake becomes defensive and walks out of the meeting. Not only has Jake missed out on an opportunity to learn from an experienced salesperson, he also risks losing his job.

In most cases of defensiveness, listeners simply aren't listening close enough. They hear criticism and blame and respond in a defensive manner. If they were truly listening, they might hear the real meaning the speaker is trying to convey.

Judging Others

Listening to another human being is a special interaction. It's a process that helps us get to know people and discover what's distinctive about them. When we truly listen to others—without making judgments about them—we begin to understand them as a unique individuals. This, in turn, enables us to form lasting relationships.

Staying Focused

Listening when it really matters can be difficult, especially when our minds are elsewhere. Here are several techniques to help you stay focused.

Maintaining eye contact with the speaker is key. This shows him or her that you're genuinely interested in what's being said. Maintaining eye contact helps keep our minds focused on what's important. It's interesting to note that in some cultures, steady eye contact is considered rude. If you think the speaker feels uncomfortable with you staring at him or her, look away, perhaps at your notes. Just don't look at the clock.

Speakers need to know listeners are paying attention to them. There are several ways for listeners to signify interest, which encourages speakers to continue. Nonverbal signals—such as nodding, leaning forward, and smiling—demonstrate interest. Watch for nonverbal signals from speakers as well. Are they smiling or frowning? Do they stutter or speak smoothly? Are they sweating? These signs allow you to gauge how a speaker is feeling.

Brief verbal signals—such as "I see," "Uh-huh," and "Go on"—encourage a speaker to continue. Asking open questions can also encourage speakers while showing your interest in clarifying their thoughts. However, be careful not to interrupt or finish someone's sentences. These things will be perceived as rude and distracting.

Last, when the speaker has finished, summarize the main point in as few words as possible. This shows that you want to avoid misunderstanding. It also reassures the speaker that you've been listening the whole time.

However, it's human nature to judge others based on things such as their speech, looks, and clothes. People often allow preconceived notions to affect their perceptions of others. We tend to classify people we don't know based on superficial criteria. When we judge people in this manner, rather than earnestly listening to their words, we can't possibly presume to know what they truly believe.

We've all heard people use labels to describe others. In fact, most of us are probably guilty of labeling people. Labels are judgments that hinder our ability to accurately assess people's genuine intentions, especially when we haven't had a real opportunity to get to know them. Labeling people is an unfair reaction. It's only when we actually listen to others that we understand their true beliefs and intentions.

"Me, Too!"

When listening to others, most people naturally compare what they're hearing to their own experiences. Even when we do our best to focus on the listener's words, our brains inevitably make connections to similar situations in our own lives. Instead of keeping these thoughts to themselves, bad listeners interrupt speakers to relate their own stories.

This type of bad listening is perceived in a number of ways, depending on the situation. "Me, too" interruptions are usually viewed as rude. Bad listeners who interrupt others to relate their own stories are making themselves the center of attention. They appear competitive to others as they try to "one up" the original speaker with a better story. In the end, when you always have a similar example to relate, others may refrain from sharing their thoughts with you at all.

People who interrupt with "me, too" stories often have good intentions. They may want to show the speaker that he or she isn't alone and that others have had similar experiences. Identifying with another person can help strengthen a relationship, especially when one person is acting as a mentor for another. The problem, however, is that the listener is presuming his or her experiences are the same as the speaker's experiences. This can be viewed as patronizing, rather than helpful. Just because a certain plan of action worked for one person doesn't mean it will work for another.

There's a right and a wrong time to compare stories. As good listeners, we need to make a conscious effort to refrain from switching the emphasis from the listener to ourselves. Following this simple rule of listening can be difficult for some, but it will help form lasting relationships with the people in your life.

"You Know What You Should Do?"

Some people feel the need to offer advice, even when no one has asked for it. As with the previous type of bad listening, advice givers presume the speaker is asking for something more than just a good listener. Simple responses of encouragement—such as "Give it some time" or "Things will get better"—merely interrupt the speaker and offer no real solution to problems.

Giving advice, instead of really listening, can become a problem when it happens frequently. A parent who constantly

Although it's a good idea to take advice from someone older and more experienced, it's important to be able to express yourself without constantly being advised what to do.

solves a child's problems fails to realize that the child won't develop real-life problem-solving skills. A boss who constantly micromanages his or her workers is not preparing them to handle problems on their own. People who are guilty of this type of bad listening need to acknowledge it as a problem and work to keep their advice to themselves until someone actually asks for it.

Being Competitive

Competitiveness in the workplace can hinder growth and productivity. This can happen, for example, when one worker becomes jealous of another's accomplishments. Let's say Ron is promoted to assistant manager, a position Christine was hoping to earn. Christine becomes angry that Ron got the position instead of her. Instead of listening to Ron during their next production meeting, Christine continually interrupts him and implies that his ideas aren't practical. Unable to continue, Ron confronts Christine about her behavior, but Christine simply denies being difficult and insists that Ron is taking the wrong approach.

It's obvious Christine is disappointed about not receiving the promotion. Instead of listening to Ron's ideas and working with the team, she selfishly chooses to make things difficult for Ron. Her competitive nature makes her a bad listener. Christine should listen to Ron's ideas, offer helpful feedback, and increase the productivity of the entire team. As a good listener, Sarah would have a better chance at being promoted the next time a position opens up.

Being Afraid

From time to time, even competent, qualified workers have fears about their job. Am I doing a good job? Does the boss like me? Will I get fired? These are natural thoughts for many people struggling to establish a successful career. However, these on-the-job fears can inhibit our ability to listen to our coworkers and bosses. For bad listeners, suggestions for improvement can sound like criticisms, making their fear of fail-ure even worse. The same can be said for students. The fear of failing a test or a class can obstruct the ability to listen during class. To a bad listener, a teacher's suggestions for improve-ment can sound like disapproval.

Fear of failure can hold us back unless we learn to relax and listen. As good listeners, we need to control our urge to panic when others offer suggestion for improvement. Even when we

Emotional outbursts are obstacles to good listening. Instead, take the time to think about what you've heard, and then ask the speaker to further clarify what he or she means.

are criticized, we need to remain calm, listen, and gather as much information as we can to improve.

Getting Emotional

Our emotions can also hinder our ability to listen effectively. We tend to misinterpret the words of others when we're angry, sad, scared, and anxious. This obstacle to listening often occurs in personal relationships, such as between friends, boyfriends

Taking the time to empathize with others by listening closely is beneficial to both speakers and listeners.

and girlfriends, and husbands and wives. These are the people with whom we usually feel the most secure. However, a lack of clear communication can cause problems in close relation-ships. Here's an example:

Joann and Marcia have been best friends for ten years. In their junior year of high school, Joann meets a boy named Sean with whom she enjoys attending school basketball games. Joann doesn't invite Marcia to go with them because she knows Marcia doesn't like sports. Marcia soon becomes sad and jealous of the closeness Joann and Sean share. She feels like Joann is dumping her for a new friend. Marcia sug-gests that she tag along with them to watch a game on Friday, but Joann says, "Don't be silly, you hate basketball." Joann certainly didn't mean to hurt Marcia's feelings, but all Marcia heard was, "Don't be silly, we don't want you around."

It can be hard to set our feelings aside. But good listeners need to do just that to make sure they get the real meaning behind what speakers are saying.

Learn to Empathize

Most of the obstacles to listening addressed in this chapter have one thing in common: they occur when a bad listener puts his or her own needs before the needs of the speaker. When we defend, we are trying to protect ourselves. When we say "me, too," we are shifting the focus of the conversa-tion away from the speaker and onto ourselves. When we give advice instead of listening, we want to present ourselves as a capable, responsible person. Each of these actions takes the

MYTHS
and
facts

ways results in negative outcome. We can't possibly understand how someone feels or what he wan just by looking at him. It's unfair judge others based on their look Always give people a chance speak before labeling them.

MYTH
Interrupting a speaker is fine as long as I have something important to say.

fact
Interrupting someone else is almost never OK. It can cause the speaker to lose her train of thought. If you do it often enough, the speaker can decide that you're not the best person to talk to. She may not share her thoughts with you in the future. If possible, always wait for the speaker to pause to ask a question or to make a comment.

MYTH
First impressions of people often lead to accurate judgments of their personality.

fact
No matter how good someone thinks they are at judging people before listening to them, labeling and stereotyping people almost al-

MYTH
A good listener remains passi and lets the speaker do all the wo

fact
Listening is an interactive proces While it's important not to interru a speaker, active listeners kno when to provide input, whether th means asking a question, para phrasing the speaker's words, giving valuable advice.

emphasis off the speaker's words, rather than focusing our attention on them.

In order to break our bad listening habits, we must set our own needs aside and concentrate on the speaker's needs. By listening, we can come to a better understanding of what the speaker really needs, whether that's a shoulder to cry on, someone to brag to, or someone to lend advice. One of the strongest characteristics of a good listener is the ability to empathize with others. Empathy is being aware of and sensitive to the thoughts and feelings of another person. When we're able to empathize with another person, we become capable of forging important and compassionate relationships.

CHAPTER 3

HOW WE LISTEN

There are plenty of wrong ways to listen, but what's the right way? Listening is more than simply being quiet. It's an interactive process that involves essential communication techniques. Good listeners know when to keep their mouths closed and when to speak.

Listening techniques can be classified into three categories: competitive listening, passive listening, and active listening. The first two types are ineffective. More often than not, they cause difficulties between listener and speaker. The third type is based on the concept of empathy. Active listening skills allow listeners to gain a deeper understanding of people.

Competitive Listening

Competitive listening is also called combative or aggressive listening. Competitive listeners are more worried about their own agenda. They interrupt speakers because they can't wait to include their opinions in the conversation. They're also likely to put others down or use sarcasm. Often, competitive listeners don't even hear what the speaker is saying because they're planning what they're going to say next. Aggressive listeners like to be right.

Competitive listeners listen just long enough to hear what they think is most important, and then they respond. They take a "win or lose" attitude, which commonly leads to fights. When there are two competitive listeners participating in the same conversation, it's rare that anyone else gets to speak.

Competitive listeners in the workplace make business difficult. Here's an example: Carlos is the assistant manager of a coffee shop. He's a hard worker and hopes to be promoted to manager. He knows he has a lot of good ideas and frequently vocalizes his feelings to the workers around him. However, Carlos has a hard time listening to others. When others try to make suggestions, he interrupts them to say why it won't work. He takes this attitude with the manager and even the owner. Carlos raises his voice to customers, puts down employees, and argues with just about everyone. Although the shop owner admits that Carlos is a hard worker with innovative ideas, she feels his poor listening skills are a detriment to the business. In the end, she decides to promote someone else. Upon hearing the news, Carlos becomes angry. He refuses to listen to the owner's explanation. Instead of calmly talking to the owner to gain a better understanding of the situation, Carlos quits and storms out of the shop.

Carlos doesn't get along with coworkers, managers, or customers. His poor attitude can only result in bad business. Not all incidents involving competitive listeners are as extreme as Carlos's story. However, this example shows how detrimental a competitive listening style can be for a worker, as well as the business itself.

Passive Listening

Passive listeners are usually interested in what others have to say, but they rarely contribute to the conversation or offer feedback. They accept what they've heard as fact and seldom ask questions to clarify what others say. Passive listeners mumble, whisper, and use facial expressions alone to convey emotions. Often, they don't say a word while others wait for them to respond. While competitive listeners tend to put their needs before the needs of others, passive listeners are meek and submissive. They rarely offer their own opinions, even when asked to

There are times when a speaker is expecting a decisive response from listeners. It can be frustrating when passive listeners fail to respond constructively.

do so. When passive listeners do respond, they often speak softly, pause frequently, and expect others to know what they mean without actually coming out and saying it. Being a passive listener on the job can be just as problematic as being a competitive listener.

Louis works for a florist in a large city. Louis's coworkers know him as a quiet guy who often keeps to himself. Although everyone gets along with him, no one knows too much about him. One morning, Louis's boss, Sandy, asks him to complete a project for an important client. Sandy asks him to create two dozen floral arrangements for a wedding that will take place in just two days. Sandy tells Louis not to use lilies, since the bride is very allergic to them. Instead of responding to his boss to verify what he heard, Louis simply nods his head and gets to work. After many hours of hard work, Louis shows the completed arrangements to his boss. Sandy is shocked to find that Louis included lilies. Louis is normally good, but this mistake is disastrous. Now they have to work overnight to correct the error and have the flowers ready for the client's wedding.

In this case, Louis could have avoided the problem by asking more questions to verify Sandy's instructions. As a passive listener, Louis nodded but failed to clarify the directions. If this type of mistake occurs again, it's likely Sandy would consider firing him.

Active Listening

Active listeners are true communicators. They're interested in hearing what a speaker has to say. Active listeners are far less likely to encounter misunderstandings than the other two types of listeners discussed above.

Active listening is not just an effective communication skill. It's also a good way to form lasting relationships.

Active listeners stand out from the other two types of listeners in several key ways. Active listeners pay deep attention to the speaker without interrupting. They ask questions to help clarify the speaker's words. They paraphrase the speaker's words to verify that they truly understand the meaning behind them. And they offer feedback if and when the speaker asks them to do so. Most importantly, they approach the speaker with an open mind and do their best to empathize with him or her. The sections that follow describe the essential components of active listening.

Focus on the Speaker

When someone is speaking, we should do nothing but concentrate on the person's words. We aren't thinking about what we want to say next or what type of advice we should give. We avoid feeling defensive and see the real meaning behind what's being said. We also push our judgments aside. Active listeners relax and open their minds when conscientiously focusing on a speaker's words.

A significant part of focusing on the speaker is not interrupting. Interrupting a speaker can cause him or her to lose the train of thought. It can also be seen as rude and cause the speaker to distrust the listener. Don't agree or disagree with the speaker, and don't rush him or her—just listen. Allow speakers to gather their thoughts and express themselves at their own pace. As mentioned previously, good listeners use quick verbal responses to encourage the speaker to continue without interrupting the flow of the words.

These students demonstrate good listening skills by smiling and staying focused on the speaker.

Focusing on the speaker can be difficult, and we may need to practice it. In time it becomes much easier. In fact, good listeners often derive great pride from being able to focus on the speaker without becoming distracted.

Body Language

Active listeners give verbal feedback to speakers to reassure them that they are listening and to clarify what they've heard. However, body language gives speakers plenty of clues about how well we're listening. Maintaining positive body language

45

can put a speaker at ease and reassure the person that we are good listeners.

The way you position your body when others are talking says a lot about your level of interest. You might, in fact, be interested in what the speaker is saying, but if your posture says otherwise, he or she might think you're bored, annoyed, or angry. Slouching can tell a speaker that you're bored or tired and probably not listening. If you're not directly facing the speaker, he or she might think you're distracted or annoyed. To maintain a positive feeling between you and the speaker, stand or sit in a relaxed position, but don't slump. Keep your body facing the speaker, and try not to sway or turn away. Eye contact is also very important during a conversation. If you're not looking at the speaker, the person is sure to think you don't care.

A listener's arms, hands, and legs can be very distracting to a speaker. Disruptive behaviors can include pointing, drumming your fingers, rubbing your hands or face, crossing and uncrossing your arms, putting your hands

on your hips, swinging your legs, and tapping your toes. Not only are these actions distracting, they show a lack of interest. Also, avoid playing with "props," such as pencils, papers, cell phones, and jewelry, during a conversation.

The young woman on the left is standing up, smiling, and maintaining eye contact. She's practicing good listening skills.

Interpret the Speaker's Words

Active listeners are constantly analyzing the meaning behind what they're hearing. Sometimes this can be a straightforward task, but other times they need to read between the lines to discover what the speaker really wants to say. Pay attention to the speaker's choice of words and the feeling with which the words are spoken. As with focusing on the listener, this, too, may seem like a difficult task, especially to someone who isn't used to doing it. However, careful listeners gradually become more compassionate to the needs of others the more they work at it. In time, this process of interpreting the words of others becomes more natural, too.

A speaker's words are the main focus of active listening, but a speaker's body language and emotions can tell the listener a lot about the person, too. A nervous speaker might have trouble sitting still or may be sweating. An angry speaker might have trouble finishing sentences. Embarrassed speakers may sit with their arms folded, or they may turn away from the listener. These nonverbal signs can help the observant listener better understand the speaker's emotional state, which can shed light on the speaker's words.

It's important to note that our interpretation of a speaker's words can be highly subjective. The meaning we get from the words of others is influenced by our own experiences and perceptions. Active listeners need to recognize that their analysis of a situation is not necessarily the correct one. This is just one more reason why focusing on a speaker's words is so important.

Asking Questions

Another good way to clarify the meaning of a speaker's words is to ask questions. This could be done at any point in the discussion, as long as the listener isn't interrupting the speaker. Oftentimes, the speaker leaves openings in the conversation to allow the listener to respond or ask questions. This gives the speaker the feedback he or she needs to continue the conversation. Asking questions also shows the speaker that you're listening and that you care about what he or she is saying.

It's important to ask open questions to prompt the speaker to continue. Avoid asking questions that make judgments, which can have a negative effect. The kinds of questions you ask will vary depending on the actual conversation. The following list contains questions a listener might ask. Which of them will help clarify what you've heard? Which of them are judgmental?

- Why do you think your mom is mad at you?
- How do you think you should proceed?
- How can you possibly do that by yourself?
- Why are you nervous about the meeting with your boss?
- Who told you it was OK to make that call?
- You said you feel terrible. What do you mean by that?
- Don't you think you could have given her more time?
- How do you feel now that you've made that decision?

From time to time, active listeners will recognize that speakers embellish or twist the truth. Some may do this deliberately to try to deceive others or to paint the situation in a light more beneficial to their own needs. Others, however, may not realize

Active listeners ask speakers to verify what they've said to make sure that they understand.

they're even doing it. The more we understand the speaker's emotions and motives, the closer we will come to truly understanding the point that he or she is trying to convey.

Verify the Speaker's Words

Throughout the listening process, active listeners usually have opportunities to verify what they've heard. This typically occurs when the speaker pauses. It's important not to interrupt the speaker. Let the person finish what he or she needs to say, and pause for at least three seconds before attempting to verify.

One of the most effective ways of verifying the speaker's words is to paraphrase what you've heard. Take the meaning that you've gathered from the speaker's words and relay it back to the person in your own words. You might say something like, "It sounds to me like you're discouraged about not making the team." Or, "If I'm hearing you right, you want me to take on some extra work for the next few weeks."

Another way to verify the speaker's words is to summarize what was said. This is similar to paraphrasing in that you are using your own words to restate what the speaker had said. However, summarizing is usually a longer and more complete synopsis of the speaker's words, from beginning to end. Usually a good listener can summarize a speaker's words in just a few sentences.

Avoid judging the speaker when verifying. By judging the speaker, the listener risks upsetting the person, and all of your careful listening may go down the drain. However, you also risk swaying the speaker into believing your interpretation instead of how he or she actually feels. Instead, simply restate or summarize the meaning of the speaker's words as you have interpreted them.

Verifying is beneficial for several reasons. It helps listeners make sure they heard the speaker correctly while encouraging the speaker to give more information. It allows speakers to restate themselves and clarify their thoughts. Verifying also shows the speaker that you're listening and want to hear more. This nonjudgmental process brings listener and speaker closer to a mutual understanding.

Give Feedback

Eventually, all speakers finish what they needed to say. What next? It depends on what the speaker was hoping to get by talking in the first place, which is what the listener needs to figure out. Sometimes the speaker just needs someone to talk to and isn't necessarily in need of a response. Other times, he or she is talking to someone with the intention of getting feedback.

Feedback could be emotional support, advice about a problem, or even just a hug to cheer the person up. Then again, it could be as simple as nodding and saying "I got it." Refrain from giving advice until the speaker asks for it. Through the process of active listening, a good listener will know how to respond.

On occasion, even the best listener won't have a definitive answer for the speaker, and that's OK. The listener may want to come out and say that, rather than giving a judgmental response. Many listeners want to reply so badly to help the speaker that they fall back on cliché answers. Saying things like "Don't worry, it'll get better" rarely makes people feel better.

Of course, not all discussions are emotional ones, and listeners are often expected to give an answer, as with people on the job. If your boss explains a new procedure at work and then asks your opinion of it, he or she is obviously in need of an answer. Again, every conversation is different, and listeners need to rely on their interpretation of each situation to dictate the feedback.

CHAPTER 4

WHO ARE YOU LISTENING TO?

By now you're ready to begin practicing active listening in your daily life. However, not all listening instances are the same. The manner in which our listening skills are put to use still depends on the individual circumstances we experience from one conversation to the next.

The way we listen to our parents is not quite the same way we listen to teachers. We listen to a friend's problem one way, and we listen to a boss's instructions another way. Different types of speakers expect or need different things from the listener. A friend may expect you to remember his or her birthday. Your boss will expect you to get to work on time. In other words, our active listening skills are influenced by the type of speaker we're listening to.

In this chapter, we'll look at specific situations where active listening will come into play and see how a listener might react differently depending on the specific conditions. By comparing both bad and good listening skills for each situation, we will better be able to apply the methods we've learned to actual conversations.

Listening at Home

Everyone first learns to listen at home, or more specifically, in the environment in which we grow up. From a very early age,

Active listening in the home is the key to forming healthy, loving relationships between parents and their children.

we're taught to listen to our parents or guardians. Parents talk to their children to instill positive values, emotions, and sensibilities in them. But they also need to provide boundaries and apply punishment for breaking the rules. Ask any parent and they'll tell you it's a difficult balancing act.

Parents who are good listeners know how to keep discussions with their children calm and productive. When parents apply active listening techniques in the home, they're able to develop deep connections with their kids. This is because active listening encourages a composed, empathetic interaction. It's perhaps most important for parents to practice active listening so that their children learn how important it is to empathize with others and become good listeners themselves.

Poor Listening

Beth's friends invited her to go camping at a park that's three hours away from her home. She excitedly tells her father, Warren, that the park has fishing, canoeing, and even a nearby water park. However, Warren has some concerns.

> **Warren:** Three hours away is kind of far to go without your parents.

> **Beth:** Julie's parents are taking us. We'll be fine.

> **Warren:** I know Julie, but I've never met her parents. I'm not sure this is such a great idea.

> **Beth:** Dad, come on. They're great, trust me.

Warren: Beth, I can't let you travel three hours away on a camping trip with people I don't know.

Beth: I can't believe this! You never let me do anything!

Warren's concerns are important, but Beth refuses to hear what he has to say. Instead, she assumes that he's being overprotective. Because of her poor listening skills, Beth becomes upset and angry, ruining her chances of going on the trip.

Good Listening

If Beth had better listening skills, the conversation may have gone smoother.

Warren: Three hours away is kind of far to go without your parents.

Beth: Julie's parents are taking us. They're very nice.

Warren: I know Julie, but I've never met her parents. I'm not sure this is such a great idea.

Beth: OK, I can tell you're concerned about my safety. What if you met with Julie's parents and talked to them? Maybe then you can decide to let me go.

Warren: That's a good idea, Beth. What's their number?

Instead of getting upset with her father, Beth remains calm. She empathizes with him so that she can better understand him and show that she cares about his feelings. She's aware of and recognizes his concern about her safety and offers a logical solution to the situation. Beth still may not go on the trip, but she increases her chances by listening to someone close to her.

Listening to Friends

Our friends are often the people with whom we share the most emotional conversations. When we're upset about something, we usually turn to our friends for comfort and advice. Likewise, when we have good news, we like to share it with our friends. We want our friends to empathize and listen to us in our time of need.

Our close friends expect us to listen this way, too. When we fail to be good listeners for our friends, they may not stay our friends for long. This advice pertains to siblings as well. Our brothers and sisters are usually close in age to us, and we often share things with them that we'd rather not share with our parents. While you can't simply stop being a brother or sister, you may lose a valuable family confidant if you chose not to listen to them in their time of need. Here's an example of poor and good listening:.

Kyle just got back from a family vacation. He's dying to tell his friend Nick all about the trip, especially how he learned to scuba dive.

Having a good friend means having someone you can tell about your accomplishments and successes. Being a good friend means doing the same for her.

Poor Listening

Kyle: It was amazing! The weather was great, and we went scuba diving almost every day. It was hard at first but—

Nick: I used to go with my Uncle Karl in Florida all the time. He's an instructor. One time we even swam right up to a bunch of dolphins! It was awesome!

Just as Kyle was about to describe his vacation, Nick interrupts to talk about his own experiences. Nick fails to focus on his friend. Instead, he allows his inner voice to take control of the conversation. Nick fails to empathize with his friend.

Good Listening

Instead of interrupting Kyle, Nick should refrain from allowing his inner voice to dictate the conversation.

Kyle: It was amazing! The weather was great, and we went scuba diving almost every day. It was hard at first, but I got pretty good at it.

Nick: Great! What was it like?

Kyle: The water was really warm. I wanted to stay under all day. We took underwater pictures of a coral reef. I'll show them to you later. I hope I get to go back again someday.

Nick: That sounds amazing. What else did you do?

Not only does Nick listen to Kyle, he encourages him to continue. This is how friends use active listening to become closer.

Listening at School

Everybody knows it can be difficult to pay attention in school. Students aren't always interested in the class topic. Outside the windows, the sky is blue and the sun is shining. The clock doesn't seem to move, probably because we keep staring at it.

Despite distractions, school can be the best place to improve our ability to focus. Similar to the relationships we share with our parents, our teachers, counselors, and coaches are there to guide us and help us build the skills necessary to make it in the world. It's in our best interest to practice focusing on these valuable sources of support and guidance.

Poor Listening

Rebecca's math teacher, Mr. Carlton, asks her to stay after class. Lately, he tells her, her grades have been slipping. He wants to know if there's anything wrong or if there's anything he can do to help.

Mr. Carlton: You received a 75 on the last quiz. That's not like you.

Rebecca: [Slouches in her chair. Looks at the clock.]

Mr. Carlton: I'd like to help you bring your grade up. There's a study group meeting today after school.

Daydreaming at school is an example of poor listening and can become a problem when exam day comes around.

We're going to work on the problems in chapter 12. Are you interested?

Rebecca: *[Shrugs her shoulders and yawns.]*

Mr. Carlton: I can also set up some extra credit work for you, but you'd have to—

Rebecca's cell phone rings.

Rebecca: Just a second. I have to answer this.

Mr. Carlton is taking the time to help Rebecca, but she's not focusing on his words. She's easily distracted, and her body language and actions show it. Not only is she missing a great opportunity to improve her grade, she's also being very rude to her teacher.

Good Listening

If Rebecca took a moment to realize what Mr. Carlton was doing for her, she might try harder to focus on what he's saying.

Mr. Carlton: You received a 75 on the last quiz. That's not like you.

Rebecca: *[Leans forward in her chair.]*

Mr. Carlton: I'd like to help you bring your grade up. There's a study group meeting today after school. We're going to work on the problems in chapter 12. Are you interested?

> **Rebecca:** So you're saying you'd help me raise my grade outside of class?
>
> **Mr. Carlton:** Absolutely. I can also set up some extra credit work for you, but you'd have to apply yourself to bring your grade up.
>
> **Rebecca:** Thanks, Mr. Carlton. I'll be here!

Instead of not paying attention, Rebecca focuses on Mr. Carlton and accepts his offer of help. Notice, too, that she uses paraphrasing to make sure she understands what he's saying.

Listening at Work

Listening to bosses and managers is not like listening to friends, parents, and teachers. Bosses aren't necessarily interested in helping their workers grow and learn the way parents and teachers are. Bosses may or may not be their workers' friends, but all bosses want one thing from their employees: they expect them to produce quality work.

Coworkers, too, are not necessarily going to be friends. This is not to say coworkers and bosses can't be friends. In fact, work environments where everyone cares about their fellow workers are often the most cohesive and productive. The bottom line, however, is that active listening is far more valuable than making friends in the workplace.

Meeting new people, as one does when beginning a new job, often leads to unfair judgments. The new girl's clothes are out of style—she must be poor. The new guy's shirt isn't ironed—I bet

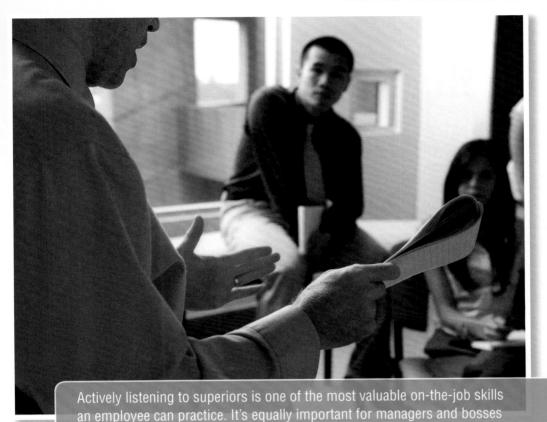

Actively listening to superiors is one of the most valuable on-the-job skills an employee can practice. It's equally important for managers and bosses to become active listeners.

he's a slob. The new boss keeps her door closed—she must not like us. Stereotyping people on the job is a dangerous trap to fall into. Our first impressions are often wrong. Continued stereotyping drives a wedge between coworkers, which will surely result in a lack of productivity. Don't make your mind up about somebody until you've had the chance to listen to him or her speak.

Managers, bosses, and coworkers aren't the only people we need to listen to at work. There are also clients, customers, patients, and many others. Making unfair judgments can ruin our chances of being successful.

Poor Listening

Abigail sells vacuum cleaners. Mrs. Schwartz, an elderly woman who lives alone, comes into her shop. Her clothes are old and worn. Her coat is ripped, and her glasses are held together with tape. Abigail doesn't think she can afford a new vacuum cleaner. She'd rather help the young couple who came in at about the same time. She's sure they'll buy a vacuum for their new home.

> **Mrs. Schwartz:** I'm thinking about buying a new vacuum cleaner, but I just don't know about these new things.
>
> **Abigail:** *[Glancing past Mrs. Schwartz, keeping an eye on the young couple.]* Well, ma'am, these machines are very expensive.
>
> **Mrs. Schwartz:** I really need a new one. I'll just look around.
>
> **Abigail:** That's fine. *[Rushes over to the young couple.]*

Abigail judges Mrs. Schwartz by her appearance without truly listening to her. This unfair assessment could have cost her a sale. To make things worse, the young couple decide the machines are too expensive for their meager budget.

Good Listening

Had Abigail used active listening with Mrs. Schwartz, her afternoon might have been more productive.

Abigail: *[Steps forward and faces Mrs. Schwartz with a smile.]* What can I do for you?

Mrs. Schwartz: I'm thinking about buying a new vacuum cleaner, but I just don't know about these new things.

Abigail: Do you have any questions?

Mrs. Schwartz: My old one just died, but I don't know if I'll understand how these new ones work. *[Checks the price tag on a nearby model.]* I can afford them, but they look so complicated.

Abigail: So the price doesn't bother you, but you think it'll be too hard to use?

Mrs. Schwartz: Yes, exactly.

Abigail: Let's look at a few machines, and I'll show you how easy they really are to use.

In this instance, Abigail gives the customer a fair chance without judging her, and it results in a sale. Abigail is especially happy because Mrs. Schwartz agrees to the extended warranty, as well as home delivery of vacuum cleaner bags. It's true that you can't judge a book by its cover. By ignoring her first impressions and focusing on the customer's words, Abigail sells a top-of-the-line vacuum cleaner.

These simple examples demonstrate the negative impacts of poor listening and the advantages of active listening. As you make a conscious effort to apply active listening techniques in your own life, you're sure to see the positive effects.

Much like being a good public speaker and a confident writer, being an active listener is a skill young people can't afford to neglect. Not only will it help you to forge lasting relationships, it also improves your chances of establishing a successful career. Active listening reduces conflicts, reinforces cooperation, and brings people together.

10 Great Questions
TO ASK A TEACHER

1. What listening tools can I use in school?

2. What does it mean to put myself in the speaker's shoes?

3. What does paraphrasing mean?

4. What can I do to listen better at work?

5. How do I read a person's body language?

6. Why is eye contact so important when listening to someone?

7. Why is it disrespectful to interrupt a speaker?

8. What do I do if I don't know the answer to a speaker's question?

9. How can labeling or judging speakers affect the way I hear them?

10. What's the difference between listening to my parents and listening to my teachers?

GLOSSARY

BENEFICIAL Good or advantageous.

CIVIL RIGHTS The rights that citizens of a society are supposed to have.

CLICHÉ A phrase or word that has lost its effectiveness from overuse.

COLLEAGUE A coworker or a fellow professional.

COMPASSIONATE Showing kindness and understanding for others.

COMPETITIVE Wanting to achieve more than others.

CONFIDANT A person someone trusts and discusses personal issues with.

CRITICIZE To express disapproval with someone or something.

EMBELLISH To make something more interesting or dramatic by exaggerating details.

EMPATHY The ability to identify with others and understand their feelings.

FEEDBACK A response to something someone else has said.

INTERACTIVE Involving communication or cooperation between people.

MENTOR A more experienced and often older person who guides a less experienced person.

MICROMANAGE To closely observe or control the work of people working under you.

PARAPHRASE To restate something using different words.

PASSIVE Not participating and letting others make decisions.

PATRONIZING Treating someone as if he or she is less intelligent than yourself.

PERCEPTION An understanding based on what someone observes.

SARCASM Words that mean the opposite of what they seem to say and are meant to mock others.

SIBLING A brother or sister.

THERAPEUTIC Tending to improve or maintain personal health.

VERIFY To check that something is true.

FOR MORE INFORMATION

Career Kids
5043 Gregg Way
Auburn, CA 95602
(800) 537-0909
Web site: http://www.careerkids.com
Career Kids offers a great selection of educational materials for
    careers, guidance, life skills, job searches, and workforce
    development.

Center for Nonviolent Communication
5600 San Francisco Road NE, Suite A
Albuquerque, NM 87109
(505) 244-4041
Web site: http://www.cnvc.org
The Center for Nonviolent Communication is a global organization
    that supports the learning and sharing of NVC and helps people
    peacefully and effectively resolve conflicts in personal, organiza-
    tional, and political settings.

International Listening Association
Dr. Nan Johnson-Curiskis
Box 164
Belle Plaine, MN 56011
Web site: http://www.listen.org
The International Listening Association is a professional organization
    whose members are dedicated to learning more about the
    impact that listening has on all human activity.

National Communication Association
1765 N Street NW
Washington, DC 20036
(202) 464-4622

Web site: http://www.natcom.org
The National Communication Association studies all forms, modes,
   media, and consequences of communication through humanis-
   tic, social scientific, and aesthetic inquiry.

Web Sites

Due to the changing nature of Internet links, Rosen Publishing
has developed an online list of Web sites related to the subject
of this book. This site is updated regularly. Please use this link
to access the list:

http://www.rosenlinks.com/cwc/lstn

Anderson, Peter. *The Complete Idiot's Guide to Body Language*. New York, NY: Alpha, 2004.

Baker, Jed. *Social Skills Picture Book for High School and Beyond*. Arlington, TX: Future Horizons, 2006.

Burstein, John. *Have You Heard? Active Listening*. New York, NY: Crabtree Publishing, 2010.

Covey, Stephen. *Daily Reflections for Highly Effective Teens*. New York, NY: Simon & Schuster, 1999.

Covey, Stephen. *The 7 Habits of Highly Effective Teens*. New York, NY: Simon & Schuster, 1998.

Diamond, Linda Eve. *Rule #1: Stop Talking!* Cupertino, CA: Listeners Press, 2007.

Donoughe, Paul J., and Mary E. Siegel. *Are You Really Listening? Keys to Successful Communication*. Notre Dame, IN: Sorin Books, 2005.

Ferguson Publishing Staff. *Communication Skills*. New York, NY: Ferguson Publishing, 2009.

Fine, Debra. *Small Talk: How to Start a Conversation, Keep It Going, Build Networking Skills—and Leave a Positive Impression!* New York, NY: Hyperion, 2005.

Fox, Sue. *Etiquette for Dummies*. Hoboken, NJ: Wiley Publishing, 2007.

Kahane, Adam. *Solving Tough Problems: An Open Way of Talking, Listening, and Creating New Realities*. San Francisco, CA: Berrett-Koehler Publishers, 2007.

Kahaner, Ellen. *Great Communication Skills*. New York, NY: Rosen Publishing, 2008.

Lewis, Barbara A. *What Do You Stand For? A Guide to Building Character*. Minneapolis, MN: Free Spirit Publishing, 2005.

MacGregor, Mariam G. *Everyday Leadership: Attitudes and Actions for Respect and Success*. Minneapolis, MN: Free Spirit Publishing, 2006.

McKay, Matthew, Martha Davis, and Patrick Fanning. *Messages: The Communication Skills Book*. Oakland, CA: New Harbinger Publications, 2009.

Miller, Patrick, W. *Body Language on the Job*. Munster, IN: Patrick W. Miller and Associates, 2006.

Reiman, Tonya. *The Power of Body Language*. New York, NY: Pocket, 2007.

Wandberg, Robert. *Communication: Creating Understanding*. Mankato, MN: LifeMatters, 2001.

Worth, Richard. *Communication Skills*. New York, NY: Ferguson, 2009.

BIBLIOGRAPHY

Center for Nonviolent Communication. "Our Founder." May 27, 2010. Retrieved March 7, 2011 (http://www.cnvc.org/about/marshall-rosenberg.html).

Center for Nonviolent Communication. "What Is NVC." December 11, 2009. Retrieved March 7, 2011 (https://www.cnvc.org/about/what-is-nvc.html).

Covey, Stephen R. *The 7 Habits of Highly Effective People*. New York, NY: Free Press, 2004.

Diamond, Linda Eve. *Rule #1: Stop Talking!* Cupertino, CA: Listeners Press, 2007.

Donoughe, Paul J., and Mary E Siegel. *Are You Really Listening? Keys to Successful Communication*. Notre Dame, IN: Sorin Books, 2005.

Encina, Gregorio Billikopf. "Empathic Approach: Listening First Aid." University of California, November 6, 2007. Retrieved March 10, 2011 (http://www.cnr.berkeley.edu/ucce50/ag-labor/7article/listening_skills.htm).

Fine, Debra. *Small Talk: How to Start a Conversation, Keep It Going, Build Networking Skills—and Leave a Positive Impression!* New York, NY: Hyperion, 2005.

Gian, Fiero. "The Art of Empathetic Listening." Ezinearticles.com, November 30, 2008. Retrieved March 13, 2011 (http://ezinearticles.com/?The-Art-of-Empathetic-Listening&id=1724083).

Kelly, Melissa. "Active Listening for the Classroom." About.com. Retrieved March 13, 2011 (http://712educators.about.com/cs/activelistening/a/activelistening.htm).

Lee, Dick, and Delmar Hatesohl. "Listening: Our Most Used Communication Skill." University of Missouri Extension. Retrieved March 6, 2011 (http://extension.missouri.edu/publications/DisplayPub.aspx?P=CM150).

McKay, Matthew, Martha Davis, and Patrick Fanning. *Messages: The Communication Skills Book*. Oakland, CA: New Harbinger Publications, 2009.

MindTools Staff. "Active Listening: Hear What People Are Really Saying." MindTools.com. Retrieved March 10, 2011 (http://www.mindtools.com/CommSkll/ActiveListening.htm).

Nadig, Larry Allan. "Tips on Effective Listening." Retrieved March 6, 2011 (http://www.drnadig.com/listening.htm).

Nichols, Michael P. *The Lost Art of Listening*. New York, NY: The Guilford Press, 2009.

Perkins, Daniel F., and Kate Fogarty. "Active Listening: A Communication Tool." University of Florida, June 2005. Retrieved March 8, 2011 (http://edis.ifas.ufl.edu/he361).

Rosenberg, Marshall B. *Nonviolent Communication: A Language of Compassion*. Del Mar, CA: PuddleDancer Press, 1999.

Schilling, Dianne. "Listening Skills: 10 Steps to Effective Listening." Women's Media, March 20, 2010. Retrieved March 3, 2011 (http://www.womensmedia.com/grow/228-listening-skills-10-steps-to-effective-listening.html).

Webb, Michael. "Eight Barriers to Effective Listening." March 2006. Retrieved March 6, 2011 (http://www.sklatch.net/thoughtlets/listen.html).

Worth, Richard. *Communication Skills*. New York, NY: Ferguson Publishing, 2009.

Zimmerman, Alan. "Talking Is Sharing, but Listening Is Caring." Changingminds.org, February 15, 2009. Retrieved March 10, 2011 (http://changingminds.org/articles/articles09/talking_is_sharing.htm).

INDEX

About the Author

Greg Roza has a long history of listening to people. He has a master's degree in English from the State University of New York Fredonia and has been working in the publishing industry for ten years. Roza lives in Hamburg, New York, with his wife and three children—all of whom he's learned to listen to with great care and understanding.

Photo Credits

Cover (foreground, background), back cover, pp. 4–5, 25, 30–31, 40–41, 46–47, 70, 71, 73, 75, 77 Shutterstock; interior graphics © www.istockphoto.com/hypergon; p. 5 © www.istockphoto.com/Eliza Snow; p. 8 Photodisc/Thinkstock; pp. 10–11 www.istockphoto.com/Thinkstock; pp. 14–15 Image Source/Getty Images; pp. 17 Hemera Technologies/AbleStock.com/Thinkstock; p. 18 Ghislain & Marie David de Lossy/Getty Images; p. 21 ColorBlind Images/Iconica/Getty Images; pp. 22–23, 55 Jupiterimages/Pixland/Thinkstock; p. 24 ©Hollandse Hoogte/Redux; p. 33 Thinkstock/Comstock/Thinkstock; p. 34 © www.istockphoto.com/Cat London; pp. 42–43 Jupiterimages/Photos.com/Thinkstock; p. 45 BananaStock/Thinkstock; p. 50–51 Comstock/Thinkstock; p. 59 © www.istockphoto.com/Izabela Habur; p. 62 Flying Colors Ltd./Digital Vision/Getty Images; p. 65 Loungepark/Stone/Getty Images.

Designer: Les Kanturek; Editor: Nicholas Croce; Photo Researcher: Marty Levick